FUI: HOW TO DESI
INTERFACES FOR FILM AND GAMES

Featuring tips and advice from artists that worked on: Minority Report, The Avengers, Star Trek, Interstellar, Iron Man, Star Wars, The Dark Tower, Black Mirror and more

JONO YUEN, HUDS+GUIS

Dedication

This guide is dedicated to my wife, Natalie. None of this would have been possible without your never ending encouragement, enthusiasm and support.

I'd also like to dedicate this to all the aspiring artists and designers reading this. I hope this guide provides you with a better understanding of the FUI industry and gives you a little boost to start you on your way. Hopefully you'll be able to help someone in return.

For information contact :
info@hudsandguis.com
www.hudsandguis.com

Book and Cover design by Jono Yuen
ISBN-13: 978-1975795122
ISBN-10: 1975795121

First Edition: August 2017

CONTENTS

FOREWORD

F UI ENCOMPASSES ANY FICTIONAL USER INTERFACE whether it's in film, games, television or otherwise. The fact that they are fictional is what makes them so special. Imagining the possibilities of how we can display or interact with information in an environment (without the restrictions of current technology) is:

a) the purest and most challenging form of UI design

b) not just UI but can also be a form of storytelling/character design

c) and are genuinely influential in the real world because when new technology does catch up (which is happening really fast right now) FUI designers have already mapped out the territory and UI designers invariably use those reference points.

INTRODUCTION

THIS GUIDE WAS CREATED TO HELP those wanting a career in designing FUI (Fictional User Interfaces) for film, television or games. It aims to provide information about how to get there, how to get started and how to become a pro.

After 10+ years in the creative industry I appreciate the power of hindsight. Having left university with no experience at all and hoping to find work, to being in the position to hire the next generation of young designers, it has become clear to me all the things I could have done differently. When I began my career I had a lot of incorrect assumptions and gaps in my understanding of the industry. I would have loved for someone to explain to me 'how to get a job', 'what a career path in this industry could lead to', 'how I would fit into the creative process' and 'what a career in design looks like'.

This guide aims to provide insights into those very questions in the field of FUI for films, television and games, with the help of some of the best in the industry. After all, who is better placed to answer these questions than the artists and innovators that made the work that inspired us in the first place?

This book is a guide, designed to do just that - guide you. There is no one formula to follow and not everyone's situation and opportunities are the same. This guide is created to help those who don't have access to mentors or wisdom from close friends. When I was just starting out, nobody in my close circle of friends and family were designers or artists and my parents were both immigrants and owned a restaurant. I would have loved to have someone guide me and answer the many questions I had.

It would have allowed me to better prepare myself for my career, or even decide whether or not I wanted that as my career. Either way that information would have armed me for whatever I decided to do. Hopefully this guide can fill that gap for you.

I'm hoping this guide will shed light on an area of design that is not very well understood, and provide a warts-and-all account of the industry, to give you an accurate and honest representation. If this guide helps just one person learn something new that benefits their career then the many months I spent putting this together will be totally worth it!

To all my subscribers, followers, and friends out there, thank you for your enduring support. It is because of you that HUDS+GUIS has continued for the past 6 years. Thanks to my good friend Julian Frost for helping me edit this book. And a special thank you to all the amazingly talented artists who have generously donated your time to contribute to this guide and shared your most valuable experiences in an effort to help others. Without your help this guide could not exist.

WHAT IS FUI?

What does FUI stand for?

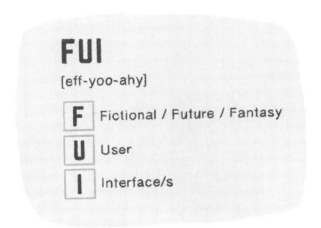

FUI
[eff-yoo-ahy]

F	Fictional / Future / Fantasy
U	User
I	Interface/s

I N FUI, THE LETTERS 'U' AND 'I' stand for 'User Interfaces'. The letter 'F' can stand for 'Fictional', 'Future' or 'Fantasy'. At HUDS+GUIS, when we reference FUI we are talking about Fictional User Interfaces.

The term 'Fictional User Interfaces' ecompasses all sorts of imaginary UI, which are usually created as part of a story. Now, these stories can be set in the future, the current day or in the past. That is why we don't limit FUI to just 'Future' user interfaces.

With regards to 'Fantasy' user interfaces, this conjures up images of the fantastical or sensational. The word 'Fantasy' is often used to describe things that are too far removed from reality, things that are unattainable. For example, the dictionary partly describes it as "a supposition based on no solid foundation". Fictional User Interfaces, however, can include UI that are based on reality and real technology.

What are Fictional User Interfaces?

If you've ever watched a Sci-Fi film or played video games before, then you're likely to have seen some form of Fictional User Interface. FUI is basically a term to describe interfaces that don't actually exist, they are imaginary. They are very common in Sci-Fi films because the stories often require UI design that is different than the current day norm. If a story was set in space or in the future, you wouldn't expect that characters to be interacting with the interfaces or devices that we use today. Therefore somebody needs to design an interface that doesn't yet exist. They need to design an FUI.

Examples of this can be seen in films like Minority Report, Iron Man, Avatar, Terminator, Star Wars, Star Trek, etc.

In fact, it is common in many Sci-Fi novels too. Whenever there is a device or interface that is made up as part of the story, that is also an FUI.

Why FUI?

Fig. 1

Fig. 2

We are interested in the way people explore user interface design outside of everyday reality. This is an extremely interesting area of UI design.

It's not often that artists get asked to design a user interface for a spaceship, time-travel device, a sentient AI or a UI in an alien language. This allows designers to push the limits of UX and UI, and explore ideas outside of the everyday. Through this task we are able to generate new ideas and new solutions that can influence or inspire real UI or even new inventions. They can act as a type of Proof of Concept. They can inspire us, raise questions, and provide examples of what works and what doesn't. Ultimately, it gets us exploring what the possibilities are.

Just as science fiction books can inspire people to fly to the moon or build self-driving cars. Fictional User Interfaces can inspire people to create technology for the future.

Minority Report (2002) is a prime example. Xbox Kinect was released in 2010, which featured a gestural interface much like the one in Minority Report. Then in 2013, Leap Motion was released and allowed you to do the same on your desktop. Now, we can't attribute those inventions purely to one source, but the scenario helps demonstrate how an FUI could inspire someone to create a similar UI for real.

What's great about FUI is that designers don't have to worry about how it's going to be built, so they're not restricted to the limitations of current technology. As a result, FUI is often the boldest, most innovative examples of user interfaces because they're only limited to the imagination. It is UI design with ultimate freedom!

CONTRIBUTING ARTISTS

W E HAVE GATHERED A GROUP OF the best artists in the FUI industry to provide depth and inside-knowledge into each section. They are a mixture of experts from film, television and games and together they help provide a comprehensive view on the industry. Here is the list of the amazingly talented artists that have generously donated their time to contribute to this guide (in alphabetical order).

Alan Torres
Design Supervisor at Cantina Creative
Credits include: Captain America: Civil War, Avengers: Age of Ultron, Fate of the Furious, Furious 7, Guardians of the Galaxy, Captain America: The Winter Soldier, Iron Man 3, The Avengers

Ash Thorp
Director / Designer
Credits include: Lost Boy, Ghost in the Shell, Ender's Game, Assassin's Creed, Call of Duty: Infinite Warfare, 007: Spectre, Total Recall, Prometheus, Robocop

Chris Kieffer
Art Director / UI Designer
Credits include: Westworld, Passengers, Interstellar, G.I. Joe: Retaliation, Deep Water Horizon, Independence Day: Resurgence, Transcendence

Corey Bramall (Decca Digital)
FUI & Motion Graphics Designer for Film & Television
Credits include: Spider-Man: Homecoming, Transformers: The Last Knight, Guardians of the Galaxy Vol. 2, Teenage Mutant Ninja Turtles: Out of the Shadows, Ant-Man, Transformers: Age of Extinction, The Amazing Spiderman

Davison Carvalho
Lead Ui Artist at Microsoft 343i
Credits include: Star Wars: The Force Awakens, Doctor Strange, Captain America: Civil War, Lone Echo, Mortal Kombat X, Paragon, Deformers

Gemma Kingsley
Graphic Art Director
Credits include: Black Mirror, The Conjuring 2, London Has Fallen

Jayse Hansen
UI Design Futurist
Credits include: Spider-Man Homecoming, Guardians 2, Star Wars: The Force Awakens, The Avengers 1&2, Iron Man 3, The Hunger Games: Catching Fire/Mockingjay 1 & 2, Big Hero 6, Star Trek Beyond, Batman vs Superman, Rise of the Planet of the Apes

Jérémie Benhamou
Lead UI Artist at Activision / Sledgehammer Games
Credits include: Call of Duty: WWII, Call of Duty: Advanced Warfare, Dead Space 2, Dead Space 3, Assassins Creed: Unity, Rainbow Six: Siege

John LePore
Principal, Chief Creative Director at Perception
Credits include: Batman V Superman: Dawn of Justice, Captain America: Civil War, Iron Man 2, The Avengers, Robocop, Thor: The Dark World, The Europa Report

Jorge Almeida
User Interface designer, animator, and fine artist
Credits include: Minority Report, Star Trek Into Darkness, The Dark Knight Rises, Mission Impossible: Ghost Protocol, Iron Man 2, Microsoft Future Vision 2015

Ryan Rafferty-Phelan
Motion Designer at Territory Studio
Credits include: Avengers Age of Ultron, Mission Impossible V, Agent 47, Guardians of the Galaxy

Now that we've done our introductions, let's get straight into answering some of our biggest questions!

WHAT IS THE PROCESS/ WORKFLOW?

O NE OF THE MOST COMMON QUESTIONS I receive is about the ambiguity of the production process, particularly within larger teams. How does a project start and finish and where will you fit into the process?

Production processes and workflows differ depending on the situation, the project and the people involved. This makes it difficult to pinpoint one definitive route to follow.

> *"As far as what you're expected to do, every film has a slightly different process."*
>
> *- Jayse Hansen*

Luckily we've been able to gather insights from a variety of artists from all around the world with different backgrounds and experiences, to help form a comprehensive answer. This won't be 'The One Answer' but rather a collection of different ways it could work.

As a starting point, here is an example of how it often works for film (could similarly work for games as well).

Example process
1. Pre-production
Brief

A creative brief is provided by the Production Designer/Supervising Art Director on the film. Sometimes the script is also provided to give a comprehensive understanding of the story. This stage could involve some back and forth until all stakeholders agree on what's required.

"First step is reading the scenes in a script that pertain the the set(s) I'm designing graphics for looking for information such as overall tone, is this future-tech, real world design or somewhere in between."

- Corey Bramall (Decca Digital)

"So, my first task is to try to understand how the director intends to use the design to move the story along. This is crucial because story is the thing that a director (and the audience) cares about most."

- Jayse Hansen

"The brief doesn't necessarily come in document form, this can be notes from a call or just some loose thoughts depending on how much information we've been given at the start to work with."

- Ryan Rafferty-Phelan

" It's usually a combination of production designer, writer, producer, director and myself who sit and discuss ideas. We find out about the product/set/prop the UI will sit on and the ideas of what that will be and how the UI will work in connection with the prop so it fits together on screen."

- Gemma Kingsley

2. Early research

Surface level style references are gathered, to collect together thoughts around mood, colour and other inspiration. This is to quickly provide thought starters and fuel discussion with the Art Director. The goal is to agree upon a direction without having invested too much time in this process.

> *"References generally serve as the foundation for communication between myself, the Creative Director and the production team based onset. These references are put together in a deck and shared with the director and their team, opening up the discussion and enabling us to get to the essence of what they want to achieve aesthetically."*
>
> *- Ryan Rafferty-Phelan*

3. Style frames

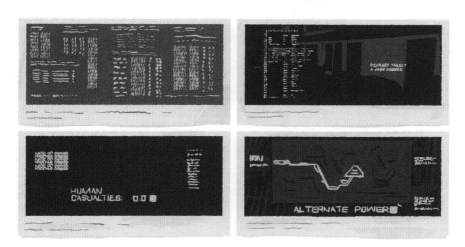

Once a rough direction is decided on, the next step is to refine it. This could involve style frames that articulate the vision and illustrate the final look of a design. This could also include motion prototypes/tests to demonstrate or explore how the designs function or move.

> *"Start putting a selection of ideas into a package and presentation, with explanations of how the technology works with the actor and how the viewer can associate with it while watching it."*
>
> *- Gemma Kingsley*

> *"This process may sometimes require jumping into animation early on so the client can get a feel for how things will move which a still frame doesn't necessarily indicate."*
>
> *- Ryan Rafferty-Phelan*

"Most people you're presenting to will not be designers. They need to see it 'in the shot' so to speak. So we'll do what's called 'tempcomps' or 'slapcomps'....This allows directors to visualize how they would film it or how it might look comped into a final shot."

– Jayse Hansen

4. Production Development

Once the design has been approved, and the director is happy with the way everything is going to fit together, the production team can then go to work at executing the various shots required. This includes creating all the animation and compositing them into the final shots. Sometimes extra animators and designers are brought in to help out. Alternatively the animations could be passed onto an external VFX team to incorporate into the final shots.

"Once stills are approved I'll animate the screens for a final round of notes. I'll then either render out whatever format the VFX vendor wants or if the designs are for production I'll make looping Quicktimes or author in Director if interactivity is required."

- *Corey Bramall (Decca Digital)*

"Executing the final shot. For me, this usually means working with a compositor to make sure the UI is sitting perfectly in the shot."

- *Alan Torres*

"Sometimes the design must change because the actions and the edit doesn't work with the edit, it makes sense on paper but not in the film, so we work together with editors to make the graphics storyline fit the film."

- *Gemma Kingsley*

🔆 Quick tip

All of this can be a little overwhelming for people just starting out, but don't let any of this intimidate you! All successful artists and designers have been in the same shoes. You will learn as you go, you don't need to know this beforehand. It is just helpful to begin to understand it. If anything, hopefully this gives you more confidence and better prepares you.

▎ Summary

- Processes can change depending on the situation, the project, and the people involved.

- 1) Pre-production: Receive the brief and get a clear understanding of what's required. This is the opportunity to question things. The goal is to get all stakeholders to agree and be on the same page from the beginning.

- 2) Early research: High level research and exploration. Start piecing together options for the art direction, without going too deep. The goal is to explore and arrive at a creative direction.

- 3) Style frames: Time to refine. This is when you take the creative direction and flesh it out, tackle specific challenges, explore motion and have a clear opinion on the art direction and design. This is usually articulated as style frames, which are still images that capture the entire look and feel of the creative direction. These frames are polished slices of exactly what the final work will look like, so that nothing is left to interpretation. The goal is to get everything fleshed out prior to the production stage, so that you can launch straight into it and start executing the final shots confidently.

- 4) Production - Execute. Take the styleframes and implement (design / animation / compositing) across all shots. The goal is to deliver the final shots.

- Remember this is just an example process, to give you a reference point. The process can change from project to project.

- One reason the above is a good process is that the clear stages allow stakeholders to understand what part of the process you're in, and have the chance to give feedback at each point. If you are working on a personal project where you're executing your own vision, the steps may blur together a bit. Or if you're working on an interactive project, there may be prototyping involved and technical limitations that feed back into the design.

- Just because it's a common way to approach things, doesn't mean it's the best way. If you can think of a better way to do things to suit your project, then do it. There are no rules and restrictions. It's a good habit to treat everything as an iterative process that you can reflect on and improve.

THE FUI TOOLSET - GET THE RIGHT TOOLS

PROBABLY THE SECOND MOST COMMON QUESTION I receive is around what tools are used to create FUI. Originally I was quite surprised how often this question kept coming up, but it makes complete sense. We are all inspired by this work and naturally we want to know how it was made. Well this section will explain just that!

In 2017 (when this guide was published), the software that artists most commonly use to create FUI are Photoshop, Illustrator, After Effects and Cinema 4D. Obviously there are other programs that allow you to accomplish similar things, and this is by no means something you must follow. Like all things, choose the best tools that work for you. This just forms a basic toolkit as a talking point to help explain what sort of work these tools are used for. But it helps to know that these common programs can allow you to create the work that ends up on the big screen or on AAA games.

What makes this combination so special is that they all work seamlessly together. For example, After Effects has the capability of recognising the Cinema 4D camera built into the program. Cinema 4D can recognise vector assets brought in from Illustrator, so you can manipulate vector shapes in 3D. That is why this basic suite of software works so well for FUI artists. You can accomplish so much with just these four programs.

Here's a breakdown of what they're primarily used for...

Photoshop (Design and compiling)

Photoshop is primarily used for design and compiling in the FUI process. It is great for assembling all your assets from other programs such as vector UI elements from Illustrator, 3D assets from Cinema 4D or photographic assets. It is also great for applying effects and colour adjustments.

For example... say we're tasked with designing an interface for a cockpit of a spaceship. We may first collect together various photographic shots of space to set as the background in Photoshop. Then we may import vector UI elements from Illustrator to arrange on the screen. We could then bring in a 3D render of an enemy ship, maybe make colour adjustments to it and make it red to indicate a warning. Whilst still in Photoshop we could add lens flares, glows and other lighting effects. By doing this, we can quickly mock up concept images that show how a FUI could look in situ.

That is just a basic example of how Photoshop can be used for design and compiling. Photoshop is very powerful and is an excellent tool for quickly establishing and playing around with looks and styleframes. It is the ideal choice for FUI artists wanting to put everything together for stills.

> *"I use Adobe Photoshop all the time, not so much Illustrator."*
>
> *- Jérémie Benhamou*

> *"Photoshop is then used to bind the graphics together, adding layers of treatment, texture, color adjustments, curves, levels etc to create the final look."*
>
> *- Ryan Rafferty-Phelan*

Great for... putting together stills/styleframes, effects, creating background assets, quick concepts, handling photographic elements, creating non-vector assets.

Illustrator
(Vector / Assets)

Illustrator is a vector based tool, and is mainly used for creating reusable UI assets. These assets can include detailed elements, grids, typographic elements, icons etc which can then be imported into Photoshop for concepts or effects, After Effects to animate or Cinema 4D to create 3D elements.

Being vector-based these UI assets can be scaled without losing quality, and the point and line information can be carried through to other programs (including Photoshop, After Effects and Cinema 4D) making this an ideal tool for creating an asset library.

Illustrator also has some powerful tools that can help arrange UI assets neatly and uniformly. You can be very precise with your points and measurements. Tools like 'Step and repeat', smart guides, outline view, and pathfinder also make life a lot easier.

> *"Illustrator. (I used to design with Photoshop, but Illustrator is truly that unlimited app you'll never regret mastering and has completely replaced Photoshop for my design phase.)"*
>
> *- Jayse Hansen*

> *"My early concepts are normally built using Illustrator, Photoshop, and After Effects. Beginning in Illustrator, I will block in shapes, and mix and match colors, fonts, etc."*
>
> *- Jorge Almeida*

Great for... creating an asset library, typography, icons, grids, UI elements.

After Effects (Motion)

When creating FUI, you can think of After Effects as a tool with a similar purpose to Photoshop mentioned above, but with motion. It is primarily used by FUI artists to compile assets that could be generated from Photoshop, Illustrator, Cinema 4D, photographic or from other sources, and are then animated.

After Effects may be used to create animated assets, which could then be handed over to VFX vendors to incorporate into the final film, or developers for the final game. After Effects is also sometimes used for motion prototypes, or used to support style frames to provide more information about movement.

Motion is such a vital element of user interfaces, particularly FUI, and After Effects is a powerful tool with which to explore that. Some people even skip the Photoshop stage, designing in Illustrator and going straight to After Effects.

> *"After Effects (Much faster than Photoshop and supports 3D cameras and a final workflow that's much better.) If you're the kind of designer that can design in Illustrator and tempcomp straight in AE, you will be a very valuable team player."*
>
> *- Jayse Hansen*

"Our typical process is to integrate elements into footage plates in Nuke and occasionally After Effects."

- John LePore

Note: The final output can be rendered from After Effects, but more often than not, FUI designers hand off their work to be integrated by specialist compositors in programs such as Nuke, Flame or Fusion.

Great for... animating assets, compiling shots, adding effects, motion prototypes.

Cinema 4D
(3D)

Cinema 4D is a pretty good 3D package for professionals and beginners alike. Having personally tried other 3D software in the past (3DS Max, Maya, Lightwave), Cinema 4D seemed to have the smallest learning curve and allowed me to get results quickly with minimal effort. I believe other 3D packages have the advantage in complex and detailed modelling and heavy rendering, whereas Cinema 4D has strengths in areas like motion graphics and FUI because it allows you to do simple things quickly. However, that is based on my personal experience and the experience of friends.

Being able to mock up assets quickly is perfect for FUI, where complex models are less important. However, it is still able to handle more complex models in the case of diagrams or schematics.

"In case of film work I spend a lot of time on 3D setting the scene, light, camera, materials and render."

- Davison Carvalho

"C4D is a 3D app made for designers by designers, and it's become the 'must-know' app for feature film FUI design. Luckily it's not too hard to learn."
- Jayse Hansen

"Cinema 4D is perfect for any 3D elements that feature in the screen, whether that's visualising something in the film or creating interesting data widgets or particle based systems."

- Ryan Rafferty-Phelan

Great for... quickly generating 3D assets, creating 3D shots, mapping 2D interfaces onto 3D surfaces.

 A quick side note

It's also worth mentioning that almost all the artists include pen and paper in their toolkit. As a fundamental of design, and a quick and portable tool, sketching is a very important aspect of concept creation and ideation. A genuinely useful tool and a time saver for professionals and beginners alike.

"I always try to sketch all my ideas out before I start

designing on the computer. Hopping onto the computer first can be limiting, and block the creative flow. This is the time I get to brainstorm and let all my good and bad ideas out on paper. My mind is often wandering during the concept phase, so sketching allows me to be passionate, and later help harness the final design."

- Alan Torres

Summary

- Photoshop is great for styleframes, adding effects and creating assets.

- Illustrator is excellent for creating UI assets such as icons, type, grids, and other various UI elements.

- After Effects is like Photoshop with motion. It's great for animation, motion prototypes and compiling shots.

- Cinema 4D is great for quickly generating 3D assets, and creating 3D interfaces.

- Choose whatever programs suit you.

- Try new tools often. New software, plugins or extensions are developed all the time so make sure to keep an eye out for tools that can improve your work or make your life easier. Don't be stagnant. The design industry changes constantly - stay abreast of it or be left behind.

HOW TO GET A JOB

WHEN IT COMES TO STARTING A career in the industry there are certain tips that apply to any type of design and then there are some that are more specific to FUI. Here we explore both types to give you the best chance at landing your dream job!

General advice
TIP #1

Get good at what you do! Dedicate yourself to your craft and work hard at continually improving.

Starting a career in the creative industry can be both exciting and daunting. It's never an easy decision to dedicate your life to something that you don't have much experience in, and at the same time wondering if you can make a living off it. So it's not a decision to be taken lightly. It requires a certain belief in yourself and a level of commitment and dedication. You can succeed if you're willing to work hard for it!

Some people in other industries may think that being an artist or a designer is easy -that you just draw and make pretty pictures all day. But the reality is that successful artists and designers are hard workers. Really hard workers. I don't say this to scare you off but to give you a realistic understanding of what a career in design looks like.

Design and specifically FUI design is a skill you can learn and get better at. The more training you have or the more hours you clock will reflect itself in your work.

> *"Work incredibly hard and dedicate your life entirely to what you love. At the end of the day, in this industry you will be judged and appraised for your level of craft and skill. In my mind, everything else comes second to that."*
>
> *- Ash Thorp*

TIP #2

Do what you love. Fill your portfolio with the type of work you want to do (even if it's non-client work, it doesn't matter). Make up a project that will allow you to demonstrate what you can offer prospective clients. It's often said: "they can't buy what they can't see."

Now if you're going to work hard and dedicate your career to something, then it'd better be something you love. This is really important. The best advice I give designers and students is to find out what you really love to do. The sooner you find out, the better it is for you and your career. Some people end up in their dream jobs by working in areas similar to it, which is fine. So naturally designers often think that perhaps they can work in a different design area first and eventually make their way around to what they really want to do. The risk is that your portfolio will be made up of the wrong kind of work. Instead, your portfolio should be made up of the kind of work that you want to attract. So it is better to spend that time getting better at what you really want to do.

There's no quicker way to get to where you want, then to head straight for it.

> *"On a least 3 occasions, I have hired someone who I have seen posting FUI personal projects on Twitter or Pinterest."*
>
> *- John LePore*

TIP #3

Share your work. Get it out there!

Once you have a portfolio filled with the work you want to do, it's time to share it. Share it with everyone, get as many eyeballs on your work as possible. You do this by posting your work on blogs, behance, pinterest, twitter, instagram, facebook - any place you can think of really. This increases your chances of the right people seeing it. When I say the right people, I mean Creative Directors or Producers or any others who are in the position to hire you or contact you. This does not guarantee a job offer but it certainly increases your chances.

> *"Be creative. Build concepts that illustrate ideas of how we communicate and interact with technology. Then share... with everyone."*
>
> *- Alan Torres*

FUI job advice
TIP #1

Familiarise yourself with the process. Reading this guide is a good start!

We've talked about the FUI production process in Chapter 1. This will be useful when discussing work opportunities with potential employers. It is much better to know that you've done your research rather than turn up unprepared.

You can take this a step further by creating projects that take you through all the steps in the process. You can do this yourself by making up your own project. There's nothing to stop you starting it right now. An important trait of any successful designer is being resourceful. Creative people have the skill of making things work no matter what is up against them. It's all about clever thinking and perseverance. So if you don't have the experience, make it for yourself.

This is a good exercise to do often. Many designers do this regularly to test ideas, create work for portfolios, to experiment or to learn new skills. It doesn't have to be a huge project, and it doesn't have to be long. It can be a couple of days, or even a couple of hours. It involves writing yourself a brief, doing research, creating style frames, and animating them. You can even composite them into footage if you want. Basically this gives you experience in the fundamental process of creating FUIs.

TIP #2

Learn the fundamentals of graphic design

You don't need formal training or a degree, but you should learn the fundamentals of graphic design. Study the elements and principles because they are the foundation of everything you do. This is easier than ever with the resources available online, whether it's articles, books or videos.

"UI art for games is all about solid design basics, graphic design skills, and how to make information visually clear for a person. It's not about the tools. Focus on that first, and dive into FX, 3D and Shiny things later, and you will be half way into not only an UI game job, but also of becoming a highly skilled artist that can adapt to whatever available tool."

- *Davison Carvalho*

"My advice for someone wanting to get into the FUI industry would be to start off by really understanding basic graphic design fundamentals. These skills will serve you throughout your career, far more than any particular piece of software currently in vogue."

- *Ryan Rafferty-Phelan*

TIP #3

Demonstrate that you can approach user interface design creatively.

It is not very interesting to see a designer who can replicate what has been done before. It is much more impactful and memorable to see a designer who approaches interface design in a unique and interesting way. The projects that catch the most attention are the unique and creative ones. Not only can you get new audiences looking at your work but it could also land you a job. There's a high chance that a studio, creative director or producer may stumble upon your work, just when they are looking for someone to help them on a project.

TIP #4
Be physically close to the industry you want to be a part of.

Now this isn't an essential step and sometimes not possible. However if you can do this it could be a good advantage.

> *"If you think you might want to do FUI design as a career my best suggestion is move somewhere that movies or games are made. I know that it's less important these days to be physically close to the work but it's still the best way to get a foot in the door."*
>
> *- Corey Bramall (Decca Digital)*

Remember to enjoy the ride. It's a fun journey and a rewarding one!

 A quick side note

You may wonder if it is possible to have a full time job designing FUI or if it is just something you do occasionally. Well it can be both. Some artists work full-time with studios that specialise in FUI for film and games (be aware that there's not an abundance of studios like this but they do exist). Some artists work full-time in UI departments of game studios.

Other artists work full-time in animation, motion graphics or VFX studios, where they work on FUI design when a project comes along that requires it.

Alternatively there are freelancers that become specialists in FUI, which allows them to work with different teams on different contracts.

There are many different possibilities. My advice would be that if you are going to dedicate your career to a specialised field, then it is vital to keep abreast of industry news. Keep adapting and stay relevant!

⟨?⟩ Questions to ask yourself

1. Why do you want to get a job in design? If you're just after a cruisy job, you're unlikely to be satisfied or successful.

2. What's unique about the way you approach design? Try to think of something that you can bring to the table that no one else can. This could stem from your personality, your interests, what you are influenced by or what you enjoy doing the most.

3. What is your idea of success? Is it landing your dream job? Working on a feature film or AAA game title? Think about what would make you happy. It could help to picture yourself as a 65 years old and ask yourself what sorts of things you would look back on and be proud of achieving.

Summary

- Get good at what you do. Be patient, your hard work will pay off.

- Fill your folio with the type of work you want to do.

- Don't expect to get lots of commissioned work when you're first starting out, but don't let that stop you. If you want to fill your folio up with work, be proactive and make up your own projects.

- Share your work. Get as many eyeballs on it as possible.

- Get familiar with the process. This will happen naturally after a few projects.

- Ground your career in the fundamentals of graphic design.

- Be creative. Try to avoid the obvious. Think of different ways you can approach your brief. Most creatives discard their first ideas as they are usually the least original. The best ideas come from digging deeper.

- Being physically close to the industry you want to be a part of can be a great way to get your foot in the door. It gives you the opportunity to meet people in the industry, who may be able to help you or give you the chance to show your work, or do internships etc.

PRO TIPS

MANY PRO TIPS, THERE ARE!

HERE ARE A FEW OF MY own tips to becoming a pro FUI designer.

1. Practice, Practice, Practice.

2. Learn how to be fast.

Keep an eye out for opportunities to be faster. I went to a doctor once and when he went to write a prescription on the computer, he'd type with his index fingers searching for the next letter as he went.

I couldn't help but imagine how much time he'd save if he'd learn to touch type. Similarly, learn shortcuts, learn the correct way to do things rather than long-winded hacks. Don't be lazy! Stay sharp! One reason it's good to be adept with software is that you'll be more willing to experiment and make changes to your artwork. If you're slow you might find yourself thinking something is 'good enough' because it'd take you too long to refine it or try an alternative.

3. Be observant.

Be aware of how humans interact with objects. Inspiration can come from anywhere. It could be from seeing someone tune an old radio, watching kids interact with toys or even watching animals at the zoo. Seeing living creatures using different methods and senses to control their environment can be a good way to think about new ways to interact with an interface.

4. Contribute something new.

Think about what is unique about you and what you'd like to bring to the table.

WHAT TO DO NEXT

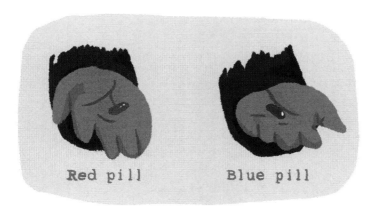

Red pill   Blue pill

G REAT JOB GETTING THIS FAR! BY this point you should have a decent understanding of the process involved in creating FUI, as well as how to create concepts and finished work and what tools to use to achieve that. We've also been through some valuable insights from some of the best artists in the industry, as well as how to get a job. So now what? How do we put this into action? Well here's what you can do right now to get started!

When talking about how to achieve your goals, some of the best tips I learnt were from a book called 'Eat That Frog' by Brian Tracy, which was recommended to me by Ash Thorp actually! I still use a lot of the tips from that book today. One of the best things the book said was to act immediately, and to do something everyday to move yourself closer to your goal. It's quite simple but it is also quite powerful, and it is something you can do.

To make this easier, we can break down tasks into **regular habits** and **long term goals**.

Regular habits

These are the tasks you should considering doing on a regular basis.

Of course you can change or add things as you please, but here are some suggestions to get you started...

- Get your skills up to scratch. Do tutorials online, practice, create mini projects for yourself.

- Identify where you can improve, make a plan on how to do it, then do it!

- Post up your work. Just get into the habit of sharing your work. There's actually quite a bit involved in this sometimes, so it's good to get used to it. Where do you want to post it? Your website, behance, instagram, twitter, facebook, dribbble?

The goal is to continue improving until your work is at the level where you will get noticed. This is what a lot of our guest artists have done themselves. It may be a long journey, but the quickest way to get there is to start straight away. The journey itself will help establish and market you as an FUI designer. Every tutorial you do, every hour you spend practicing takes you one step closer towards your goal!

"Learn as much as you can from every source you can find. Always grow."

- Jayse Hansen

"Your portfolio is the most essential tool you have in getting yourself a job. Make sure you have a website and it is up to date. Leave out the old bits that don't reflect your current abilities and try to make sure that the bits that do reflect the type of work you'd like more of, are front and centre stage."

- Ryan Rafferty-Phelan

"Only put work in your folio that you really really like, even if it's just 3 beautiful images. If you put a lot of work in, people will remember the stuff that isn't so good and most likely forget you. If you only put a few key great images in, you will probably get a call. I get portfolios full of stuff and honesty most of it is not great, if i got a 3 really cool images, I'm more likely to call you."

- Gemma Kingsley

Here's a quick tip

Give yourself mini goals that are achievable. This could be to do one tutorial a day or one mini project per month. But be diligent and try not to miss even one day or month. By the end of the year, the results will be obvious!

Long term goals

Another great piece of advice that I still refer to today, was from a teacher of mine whilst at university. He encouraged me to write down what I wanted to accomplish by the end of the year and prioritise them by putting a number next to each one. That could include things like 'work with talented people', 'work on great clients', 'work abroad', 'start a family' etc. Then with the same list, update the numbers based on what my priorities were in five years time, and then ten years time. It was clear how my priorities changed, and it gave me a clear vision of where my life could be. All of a sudden that reality became possible. I knew the things I needed to concentrate my energy on right now, but it allowed me to not lose sight of the big picture.

Plan it out (5 - 10 mins)

Grab a piece of paper or open up a simple text doc or Google doc. Write down what you want to achieve by the end of the year (or next year if it's nearly the end of the year). Try to break it down into individual goals for example, instead of 'work at my dream job' it could be things that make up a dream job like 'work with artists that I admire', 'work on a feature film', 'earn a good salary' etc.

Now write down what you want to achieve in five years time. Then the same for ten years time. You can even write down how old you will be by then.

This will become your roadmap! You may not achieve all the things you want but that's expected especially if you include stretch goals that you probably won't get to in time, but would be amazing if you did. It's like that saying of Norman Vincent Peale's: "Shoot for the moon. Even if you miss, you'll land among the stars."

I do this every year or so, to realign myself and have a clear goal to aim towards.

Hopefully by now you should feel empowered, I'm excited for you! Congratulations, you've taken a few steps closer towards becoming a professional FUI designer!

> "It's a great time for it. The demand is just starting to grow so much and will only continue. So many games, films, tv shows, commercials (and AR+VR) are relying on this type of design and animation to tell their story."
>
> - Jayse Hansen

Get started

1. Plan out your 1 year, 5 year and 10 year goals
2. Write down and commit to your regular habits
3. Think of some mini-projects you'd like to attempt
4. Take steps every day towards your goal
5. Think about what you can offer, think about something unique
6. Get to work straight away!

(?) Questions to ask yourself

1. **What are your strengths and weaknesses?** Be honest. Self-reflection is an important part of growing and developing as a person and as an artist.

2. **If you could do one personal project, what would it be?** Keep this simple and small to begin with. Don't jump into the deep end just yet! Work up to it. I suggest keeping it really simple, something you can achieve in a weekend. They can become more elaborate with each passing year.

3. **What is your first impression to the rest of the world?** Try Googling yourself and see what comes up. As you develop your work further and create an online presence by creating a folio and posting up work, you will start to leave your mark. Think about how you want to be perceived. 'A specialist FUI designer?', 'a game UI specialist?' or 'an FUI designer and animator?' It can be whatever you want.

Summary

- Commit yourself to a journey of self-improvement. Stay relevant and stay sharp!

- Identify areas where you need to improve, figure out how to strengthen those areas, then go do it!

- Share your work. You can always keep replacing old work with new work, but get into the habit of sharing your work. It takes time for things to gain traction, even for your portfolio to start ranking. It's good to get started early.

- Set yourself small regular tasks that continually improve your skills. Keep at it, don't slip even once!

- Set your long term goals. Take time to determine what your target is, and don't lose sight of it.

- Reassess your long-term goals regularly. I usually do this before the end of the year. You can see what goals you've been able to achieve and also realign yourself. Life can be unpredictable and so sometimes your priorities change. Update your goals to reflect this.

- Get on with it! Do something productive every day! I can't wait to see what you come up with!

CHECKLIST: APPROACHING YOUR INTERFACE

HERE'S A LIST OF QUESTIONS YOU can ask yourself when first approaching an interface design. These will help clarify your purpose and help inform your decisions later down the track.

1. What is the interface for? What function does it serve?

Thought starters: Is it a personalised interface? Is it for medical purposes, or military or scientific? Is it just a petrol pump to refuel a car? Be clear on the interface's reason for being.

Our example: It's an interface for a car. It helps the driver navigate to a destination, whist highlighting obstructions and damage reports on the car.

2. Who is the user?

Thought starters: Someone technically trained? Someone who's not very tech-savvy? Just one person? Multiple users simultaneously?

Our example: Predominantly the driver, who controls the settings.

3. Who sees it?

Thought starters: Co-pilot? Other doctors? The rest of the team? No one else, just the user?

Our example: The driver and front passenger.

4. Where is the interface?

Thought starters: Moving vehicle? Hidden lab? Office? Home? Somewhere personal and private? Somewhere public? What time of day is it?

Our example: A fast moving car at night. On the windscreen, possibly the mirrors and side windows too. Maybe there are controls on the dashboard or the steering wheel itself.

5. Is the interface crucial to the story?

Thought starters: Does it need to progress the plot? If so, what is does it need to communicate? What story does it need to tell?

Our example: Yes, it needs to show that our heroes are close to their destination but the car is badly damaged and about to run into some major obstacles.

6. How do you control the interface? What interactions would you use?

Thought starters: Touch, gesture, voice-control, physical dials and knobs, a separate controller, plugs into your consciousness (*The Matrix, Ghost in the Shell*)?

Our example: Primarily voice control so the driver can keep their hands on the steering wheel. Some physical buttons on the steering wheel itself.

7. How does it work?

Thought starters: How does it gather information, how does it present that back to the user? Are there limits to what it can do? Is it constantly updating?

Our example: It scans the environment several metres ahead and relays the information back. It analyses the situation and suggests alternate paths to avoid damage.

8. How does it animate? Can the animation afford any meaning?

Thought starters: Consider the mood you are trying to convey. Can you give the interface more personality by the way it moves or responds. Can the animation be used to help guide the user or the viewer? Can it be used to help explain how the interface works?

Our example: Animation is quick-paced to give the driver as much time as possible to react. Movement is used to lead the driver's eye around the screen. Urgent messages are obvious and hard to miss.

9. What would it sound like?

Thought starters: Consider the environment, is it quiet or noisy. Is sound even required? If so what role does audio play - is it just for input feedback or can it enhance the mood or even help accentuate the UI?

Our example: Sound is pretty important for the driver so the interface will only use sound in the most urgent circumstances.

For regular situations, perhaps there's a voice-over assistant like Siri.

10. What challenges do you have to deal with? How can you get around them?

Thought starters: Things you may need to consider is how long the interface will be shown on screen (for film/TV), whether it's being played back live during production or incorporated in post, what dimension screens you have to deal with or other challenges that may be worth addressing at this early stage.

Our example: The interface can't be obstructing the driver's view. The challenge will be to make the interface elements obvious enough, whilst allowing the driver and the viewer to see the road ahead. Perhaps the UI could be augmented into the environment? Also need to consider lighting and reflections.

These are just some questions that may help get you started and give you more clarity on the interface you are about to design. It will help give the interface a real purpose for being and may help inspire nuances and inform design decisions further down the track. As you use this, you may think of more questions to ask yourself. Add them to the list! Change the list! It's entirely up to you. There are many ways to approach designing FUI, and through time hopefully you can create your own ways that suit you best!

Design considerations

It is also worth considering some of the fundamental design elements and principles that make up your interface. Have a think about how you can use each of these attributes to give your interface maximum effect.

For example:
- Line
- Shape
- Form
- Colour
- Texture
- Balance
- Proportion
- Space
- Hierarchy
- Typography

CHECKLIST: ASSESSING YOUR INTERFACE

HERE ARE SOME COMMON QUESTIONS TO ask yourself when assessing your interface. Not all points are relevant all of the time. But it may be helpful to see if your interface is working as hard as it can.

1. Does your interface achieve the goal it's set out to do?

If not, refer back to the brief and the purpose for creating this interface.

2. Is it believable? Or does it stick out like a sore thumb?

In FUI, the last thing you want is to pull the audience out of the world, because the interface is completely unbelievable, too far fetched, obnoxious or just doesn't fit well into the world around it.

3. Does it fit within the world it exists in?

Is it possible for this interface to be built by someone from this world?

4. Does it fit within the environment it is in?

Does the interface feel like it suits the environment? Is it in a low-lit environment and therefore requires more contrast? Is it in a science lab and therefore quite functional or sophisticated? Is it in an old abandoned ship and therefore glitchy and out-dated?

5. Is the interface appropriate for the intended user?

Who made this interface and for whom? Is the language appropriate for the user? Should it be in English or another language? Should it be in colloquial terms or can it use acronyms for a more specialised user? Is the interface intuitive or is it designed for a power user?

6. Is it obvious what it's used for?

You can ask someone completely removed from the design to have a look and see if they can guess what the interface is for. Sometimes it is better to pare down the design to begin with, make sure that it communicates what it needs to before adding in detail and polish. There's no point designing something beautiful that fails to communicate what it is required to.

7. Is it readable, within the time it is shown?

An interface can be really well thought out, but if you only have a few seconds to see it, it might be all for nothing. Consider how to prioritise your shots to get the biggest bang for your buck!

8. Does the interface tell you something about who made it, or who it's made for?

This can elevate your interface to another level! There are opportunities to add more meaning to your UI, which will in turn make it more believable.

A good example of this can be seen in Batman Vs Superman: Dawn of Justice by Perception. There's a clear difference between Batman's (hero) and Lex's (villain) UI. The UIs are either built by them, or specifically for them so you can tell more about their personalities by the way they're designed.

9. Is the animation adding anything?

Is it paced correctly to represent the tone of the interface? Does it help direct the eye to where you want it and when you want it? Does it give you a clue into how the UI works or reflect the environment it's set in? There is a huge opportunity to convey an extra level of information by the way something moves. Make sure you use it to your advantage!

INTERVIEW: ALAN TORRES

DESIGN SUPERVISOR AT CANTINA CREATIVE

Born and raised in Oxnard, CA. Graduated from Otis College of Art and Design. Design Supervisor at Cantina Creative in Los Angeles.

Credits include: Captain America: Civil War, Avengers: Age of Ultron, Fate of the Furious, Furious 7, Guardians of the Galaxy, Captain America: The Winter Soldier, Iron Man 3, The Avengers

Website: tartvfx.com
Twitter: twitter.com/tartvfx
Instagram: instagram.com/tart85
Vimeo: www.vimeo.com/tartvfx

What does your typical process/workflow look like when creating FUI?

Phase 1 - Listening and understanding the needs of the story, its contextual placement, the objective of the interface, what sort of tech it's being applied to, and the world we are designing for. I think of these interfaces just like characters and develop them as such. Allowing me to develop a human-based experience in a given fictional/fantastic world.

Phase 2 - I always try to sketch all my ideas out before I start designing on the computer. Hopping onto the computer first can be limiting, and block the creative flow. This is the time I get to brainstorm and let all my good and bad ideas out on paper. My mind is often wandering during the concept phase, so sketching allows me to be passionate, and later help harness the final design.

Phase 3 - Building out FUI assets and framework in PS, AI and AE. It's during this phase I start thinking about color, and how I want it to drive the character, and the story of the design.

Phase 4 - Designing the style of animation and behavior of the FUI. How these assets move, is critical to the drama and clarity of the story. Also, during this phase it is beneficial to start integrating your design into the plate, to approximate how it will play in the shot.

Phase 5 - Executing the final shot. For me, this usually means working with a compositor to make sure the UI is sitting perfectly in the shot.

What is your typical FUI Toolkit?

I enjoy creating these FUI's from scratch. This helps to create a unique and identifiable aesthetic for myself. However, if time does not permit, I have an asset library that I have generated over the years, where I can pick and choose from.

a) How do you create your concepts? What tools/software do you use?

Pencil and paper, Photoshop, Illustrator, After Effects, Maya, Cinema 4D

b) How do you create the final execution of the UI or animation that goes to screen? (Or do you hand it over to another team?)

I will design, animate, then hand off the approved assets to the VFX team for the final execution.

How do you get a job designing FUI?

Be creative. Build concepts that illustrate ideas of how we communicate and interact with technology. Then share...with everyone.

What is one pro tip you would share?

I'll leave you with a quote from one of my hero designers.

> *"The team that makes the most mistakes, wins."*
> *- Tinker Hatfield*

INTERVIEW: ASH THORP

DIRECTOR / DESIGNER

My passion for art, combined with a love of feature films, naturally led me to pursue a career in the film industry. I've contributed to the design direction and concepts for Ender's Game, Total Recall, Call of Duty, Spectre [James Bond], Person of Interest, Prometheus, and many more games and films. In 2015, I co-founded and launched Learn Squared, an online educational platform for creatives with a core mission to provide affordable, quality instructional programs worldwide. I also created and host The Collective Podcast, which is aimed at exploring the struggles of work/life balance and to share the experiences of influential creatives within our community.

Credits include: Lost Boy, Ghost in the Shell, Ender's Game, Assassin's Creed, Call of Duty: Infinite Warfare, 007: Spectre, Total Recall, Prometheus, Robocop

Website: ashthorp.com
Facebook: facebook.com/ashthorpart

Twitter: twitter.com/ashthorp
Instagram: instagram.com/ashthorp
Behance: behance.net/ashthorp
Vimeo: vimeo.com/ashthorp
Store: shop.ashthorp.com
Learn squared: learnsquared.com
Lost Boy: lostboyworld.com

What is your typical process/workflow for creating FUI? (Is it different for Film and Games, since you've done both?)

My process changes for each project, as I usually like to start completely clear-minded and approach everything as if it were the first time I have worked on something in this field. I feel I owe this to the client to think of the projects in a new mindset each time. Regardless of the media, I treat both film and games the same, open-minded and focused on finding a new design perspective from what they are used to.

What is your typical FUI Toolkit:

a) How do you create your concepts? What tools/software do you use?

As I mentioned, I try and switch things up for each project, but will commonly find myself sketching out ideas and rough concepts in my sketchbook in the beginning. From there, I'll start building vector assets in Adobe Illustrator and then compiling them in Photoshop. Most recently, I have been doing render tests using

Cinema 4D and Octane to give another layer and dimensionality to some of my designs.

b) How do you create the final execution of the UI or animation that goes to screen? (Or do you hand it over to another team?)

When projects are under an extremely tight schedule, they will either provide a VFX vendor or I will enlist the help of another fellow creative for animation. Separating these tasks allows me to focus on my passion for ideation, design, direction and client relations.

How do you get a job designing FUI?

I am now fortunate enough after many years of hard work to have established great client relationships that lead to repeat business or produce referrals for new clients.

If a new designer is trying to enter this industry, the best advice I can give is to simply love what you do. Work incredibly hard and dedicate your life entirely to what you love. At the end of the day, in this industry you will be judged and appraised for your level of craft and skill. In my mind, everything else comes second to that.

What is one pro tip you would share?

Understand the power of managing your time. The richest and poorest person both share the same currency called time. What you do with your time defines your overall success in life. If you can harness that power, you will live a prolific life worth living.

Final thoughts

If you are interested in FUI or getting into the industry doing work similar to me, please feel free to join one of my classes at Learn Squared (www.learnsquared.com). In my courses, I share the step-by-step process and methodologies I have developed over the years working in the industry.

INTERVIEW: CHRIS KIEFFER
ART DIRECTOR / UI DESIGNER

Hello, my name is Chris Kieffer and I specialize in Art Direction/ UI Design. Currently I'm working at Warner Bros Studios. Some recent/ongoing Feature Film & Television projects are: Pacific Rim 2, Godzilla: King of Monsters, Rampage and The Dark Tower.

Credits include: Westworld, The Dark Tower, Passengers, Interstellar, Godzilla: King of the Monsters, Deep Water Horizon, Independence Day: Resurgence, Transcendence

Website: chriskieffer.com

What is your typical process/workflow for creating FUI for a TV series?

Usually I start by getting a script. I will read the script and do a rough breakdown. A breakdown can include everything from designing UI, Designing UI for props, On-set playback, Equipment for playback, and so on. Then I usually meet with the production designer and art director. They go over the sets, props, screens, and designs they may already have. Then I can work on refining the Breakdown. Then "Depending on the team" I would delegate who is working on what parts of the show. For example, I myself and another artists would start designing the UI, while I have another start planning on how to program all the on set playback and interactivity.

What is your typical FUI Toolkit?

    a) How do you create your concepts? What tools/software do you use?

My main toolkit is Adobe After Effects, Photoshop, Illustrator, and Cinema 4D. I use others when needed, but those are key.

    b) How do you create the final execution of the UI or animation that goes to screen? (Or do you hand it over to another team?)

That depends...
On-set playback UI deliveries are different than post. For playback there is a mix of quicktime loops, Interactive playback files that are created in Director, Flash, Animate etc. We also use software we have developed to playback graphics on screen.

In VFX, It's a mix per project. Sometimes we just create the elements that will be replaced in post by a compositor. so we will send a quicktime or image sequence. Other times we will finish the shot and deliver the final DPX sequences.

How do you get a job designing FUI?

I never set out to get a job designing FUIs. I have always been inspired by them, and what goes into making them. I started out doing motion graphics in the film industry, and that turned into designing and animating FUIs over time. The more I did them, the more I went after those types of jobs.

What is one pro tip you would share?

Practice and try designing out of your preference or style. You learn new and sometimes better ways of doing things. Force yourself into that uncomfortable zone of not knowing how something may turn out. You'll be surprised with what you can come up with.

INTERVIEW: COREY BRAMALL (DECCA DIGITAL)

FUI & MOTION GRAPHICS DESIGNER FOR FILM & TELEVISION

My name is Corey Bramall. I live in Vancouver, Canada and have been designing FUI for film and television for the past 14 years. My work has been seen films such as Captain America: Civil War, Ant-Man, 5th Wave and Transformers: Age of Extinction as well in many television shows such as X-Files, Wayward Pines and Extant.

I find inspiration for my work in architecture, photography and music. I am honored to be part of the FUI community as it grows bigger and better than I could've ever imagined a decade ago.

Credits include: Spider-Man: Homecoming, Transformers: The Last Knight, Guardians of the Galaxy Vol. 2, Teenage Mutant Ninja Turtles: Out of the Shadows, Ant-Man, Transformers: Age of Extinction, The Amazing Spiderman

Twitter: twitter.com/decca_digital
Behance: behance.net/deccadigital
LinkedIn: linkedin.com/in/coreybramall

What does your typical process/workflow look like when creating FUI?

First step is reading the scenes in a script that pertain the the set(s) I'm designing graphics for looking for information such as overall tone, is this future-tech, real world design or somewhere in between. Many times I'm given reference images by the production designer that provide color and content cues but I'll also pull my own reference as well. Once I have a basic idea of what designs are needed I'll start producing stills for approval. This stage doesn't really have any of the specific elements needed for a scene but is more of an overall look and feel for the entire set. Once stills are approved I'll animate the screens for a final round of notes. I'll then either render out whatever format the VFX vendor wants or if the designs are for production I'll make looping Quicktimes or author in Director if interactivity is required.

What is your typical FUI Toolkit?

a) How do you create your concepts? What tools/software do you use?

I'll design stills mainly in Photoshop and sometimes Illustrator and animate in After Effects. If any 3D is required I'll use Cinema 4D.

b) How do you create the final execution of the UI or animation that goes to screen? (Or do you hand it over to another team?)

I don't do any compositing so if I'm producing designs for post production I'll send file sequences to whoever the vfx vendor is on that movie and they'll do the compositing. When designing screens for production I'll typically design, animate and author each screen myself but I have on occasions also animated another designers UI elements or had one of my designs animated by another artist.

How do you get a job designing FUI?

If you think you might want to do FUI design as a career my best suggestion is move somewhere that movies or games are made. I know that it's less important these days to be physically close to the work but it's still the best way to get a foot in the door.

What is one pro tip you would share?

1. There's WAY less time to concept and design than you think. Learn to cut corners without compromising quality.

2. Under promise, over deliver.

3. Not all FUI is sexy sci-fi HUDs. All those web searches, printing dialogue boxes and cell phone displays have to be designed too so at times you'll need to be able to find inspiration within some fairly bland work.

INTERVIEW: DAVISON CARVALHO
LEAD UI ARTIST AT MICROSOFT 343I

I'm an art enthusiast and self-taught artist, always on the move and always learning.

Credits include: Star Wars: The Force Awakens, Doctor Strange, Captain America: Civil War, Lone Echo, Mortal Kombat X, Paragon, Deformers

Website: hellodave.co
Twitter: twitter.com/weeneeds
ArtStation: artstation.com/artist/weeneeds

What does your typical process/workflow look like when creating a game UI?

UI for games are different from UI for films and websites, it requires the same high quality visual treatment as film UI, but with even more interactivity than a website UI, making me think dynamically at all times. UI in games are a visually morphic tool to help tell a stories and carry a person from point A to B. And almost always less UI is ideal for storytelling.

Knowing that, my process is...

- Identify what type of audience is going to see/use an UI
- What is the purpose for a particular UI
- Identify the point A to B or a story to be expressed in that UI
- Basic UX planning in order to understand limitations, tech resources,
- Possibly prototype something (usually UX guys do this)
- Identify the Art style of the game, get art references from the actual game, like concept art, props, environments
- Collect references from other things, usually not other UI, that can influence you too much. Since maybe be too close
- Make the art and have fun on this
- Make basic implementation on Game Engines

What is your typical UI Toolkit?

a) How do you create your concepts? What tools/software do you use?

For games: If I have a clear goal in mind I just dive into Illustrator and starting making stuff, if I don't have a clear idea then I'll usually make quick 2D studies, either on illustrator / Photoshop or paper.

For films: I always start sketching quick Ideas and thumbnails, considering the photography, camera angles, light and story.

I spend 70% of my time on 2D design, before moving to the 3D part, where I make quick models to support the UI designs > In case of film work I spend a lot of time on 3D setting the scene, light, camera, materials and render.

Tools: Adobe CC (Illustrator, Photoshop, After Effects, Bridge). Modo, Houdini, World Machine, Vue, Maya, Substance Designer, Zbrush.

For games, there is also work on game engines: Unreal Engine 4 and proprietary engines modified from 3D softwares like Maya.

b) How do you create the final execution of the UI or animation that goes to screen? (Or do you hand it over to another team?)

For animation, I use After Effects for flat 2D elements, sometimes, flash or blend, but that's changing. When it's 3D I animate some basic things on Modo or a game engine, but it's just for reference to others I'll hand it over. Usually I hand it over to animators, programmers or tech artists.

What's the best way to get a job designing UI for games?

UI art for games is all about solid design basics, graphic design skills, and how to make information visually clear for a person. It's not about the tools. Focus on that first, and dive into FX, 3D and Shiny things later, and you will be half way into not only an UI game job, but also of becoming a highly skilled artist that can adapt to whatever available tool.

Making a game is usually a collaborative effort, so even if you are shy and a bit of a nerd like myself, learn the value of teamwork, interact with other artists on the internet as practice, make some collab projects together, and learn how to receive criticism in a positive and educational way.

Also be prepared to take art tests, that's a regular process for game jobs.

What is one pro tip you would share?

Achieving a great, unique and original high quality work is very hard and takes time, don't rush, don't give up on hard things for some easy way out. Power through learning hard things, move forward. Once you achieve the level or work that open doors for you, enjoy it! But prepare yourself for Reset > Update > Repeat. Learn how to evolve, how to transform your professional self from time to time. Re-cycle yourself often.

Final thoughts

Thanks Jono and HUDS+GUIS, for what I consider a public service you provide us, which is this source of inspiration and information for all pros and aspiring interface fellas! Thanks!

INTERVIEW: GEMMA KINGSLEY
GRAPHIC ART DIRECTOR

Gemma Kingsley is a freelance Designer/Graphic Art Director living and working around West London. Working primarily within the Art Department or VFX Department on film and drama productions as a Graphic/VFX Art Director or Graphic Artist depending on the job requirements.

Her responsibilities have ranged from designing and producing print graphics to assistant supervising VFX on set. So far, Gemma has been privileged enough to work over Film, Drama and Commercial productions for companies such as Universal Pictures, Warner Brothers, Working Title, BBC, ITV, Channel 4, and SKY.

In between Film/Drama jobs she also regularly works at Sky Sports.

Credits include: Black Mirror, The Conjuring 2, London Has Fallen

Website: gemmagrace.co.uk

What is your typical process/workflow for creating FUI for a TV series?

- Usually, we read the script. See what the requirements are. Talk with the writer (usually he has an idea in mind of the type of thing he is writing about, so it's a good start) and the director. It's usually a combination of production designer, writer, producer, director and myself who sit and discuss ideas. We find out about the product/set/prop the UI will sit on and the ideas of what that will be and how the UI will work in connection with the prop so it fits together on screen.

- We start researching and designing a look and feel of the UI based on concepts of the film, taking references from future/past and present technology. It's all fiction so it doesn't matter if the the technology doesn't exist, it doesn't have to, we just have to make it look like it could work.

- Start putting a selection of ideas into a package and presentation, with explanations of how the technology works with the actor and how the viewer can associate with it while watching it.

- We may do test shoots/photos for the concepts to put the graphics on, animate them into shot so it's almost like a previz of how the UI works on screen. It's all very basic but the writer and director can begin to understand how it works on screen and how the actors will work with it. We make changes, additions based on this design process. We may put a little edit together of this too.

- I usually get an overall look together of the key elements of the UI signed off. We then start shooting and things obviously change and adapt but we start working with some of the rushes - (live action plates) to see how it's working on screen (again it's more of a previz thing, so not properly tracked into shot etc).

- do a breakdown of the shots based on the script to work out a shot count for the VFX producer.

- I then work on set with the director and actors and choreograph the movements with them in relation to the UI, show them the graphic and how it will work and watch them for the correct movements so the animation works (not too fast and not too slow) - the actors can't see what they are working with so this is where being on set is very important and can save a lot of money in reshoots!

- once the shoot is done with, we start getting a rough cut of the edit. We start matching the animation (some design can sometimes change, but usually this is minimal), the shot count, usually changes. I go to meetings based on new cuts of the edit with director, producer, writer and we discuss changes and new additions to make the storyline flow correctly. Sometimes the design must change because the actions and the edit doesn't work with the edit, it makes sense on paper but not in the film, so we work together with editors to make the graphics storyline fit the film. We begin to finalise the shots as the story fits with the UI and THEN send them to a external VFX vendor to do the roto/tracking and finishing touches to the UI onto the edited live action plates. We monitor what they do to make sure the 'look' doesn't change, and give feedback in relation to this.

What is your typical UI Toolkit?

a) How do you create your concepts? What tools/software do you use?

Usually a combination of Photoshop, Illustrator and then After

Effects. Sometimes some 3D depending on what we want. Video and stills usually.

b) How do you create the final execution of the UI or animation that goes to screen? (Or do you hand it over to another team?)

Use After Effects to compile all final animations.

Occasionally use Cinema 4D to set up cameras and 3D assets, depending on the requirements.

Towards the end we hand over a few of the animations to the VFX vendor and make changes as they need them. The animations are usually timed to the cut (with frame handles) and sometimes this is still getting tweaked by the editor, so changes.

How do you get a job designing FUI for TV?

It's tough, you get rejected constantly. I kept trying really, kept contacting people I wanted to work with basically, keep reminding them that you exist and want to work with them, they are usually the best and very busy so will forget. If you keep trying they eventually may just call you back (obviously within reason!). I did jobs that didn't pay as well sometimes but the work was great, then it just turns around and you get people calling you and the pay becomes what your rate requirements are, sometimes you have to go down to go up, if you understand what I mean by that.

Only put work in your folio that you really really like, even if it's just 3 beautiful images. If you put a lot of work in, people will remember the stuff that isn't so good and most likely forget you. If you only put

79

a few key great images in, you will probably get a call. I get portfolios full of stuff and honesty most of it is not great, if i got a 3 really cool images, I'm more likely to call you.

What is one pro tip you would share?

Think outside the box. I got my first job at SkyTv based off the manager of the design department seeing my work at a high exhibition full of university students. There were hundreds of people there showing work that was far superior to mine. My technical abilities are not as strong as many others and back then it was even less, but my ideas were completely different to the others and this is why she chose my work along with 3 others. She told me, I can teach you to use the software but I can't teach you to think differently...

INTERVIEW: JAYSE HANSEN
UI DESIGN FUTURIST

From holographic interfaces to advance computer screens Jayse Hansen's work has played a defining role in major film franchises such as Star Wars, The Hunger Games, Iron Man, The Avengers, Spider Man, Guardians of the Galaxy, Ender's Game, Big Hero 6 and more.

He also consults for real-world software companies in VR and AR, as well as the Department of Defense on strategies to use his 'outside-conventional-limits' design-thinking to dramatically increase efficiency, comprehension and action when dealing with immense amounts of time-sensitive, mission-critical information.

He has delivered keynotes all over the world about his film work and next-generation UI design philosophies.

Credits include: Spider-Man Homecoming, Guardians 2, Star Wars: The Force Awakens, The Avengers 1&2, Iron Man 3, The Hunger

Games: Catching Fire/Mockingjay 1 & 2, Big Hero 6, Star Trek Beyond, Batman vs Superman, Rise of the Planet of the Apes

Website: jayse.tv
Twitter: twitter.com/jayse_
Instagram: instagram.com/jayse_
Pinterest: pinterest.com/skyjayse

What does your typical process/workflow look like when creating FUI?

It varies from film to film, but it's basically:

Lookdev - create the design look and feel
Understand/Dream/Research
Design in Illustrator
Animate the Illustrator elements in After Effects
Comp in After Effects to present in a way that sells your design ideas
Evolve - Film UI is an iterative design process.
Iterate to mature the design
Comp/Final/Deliver from After Effects

To elaborate a bit:

Understand
Directors are trusting you with some important parts of their story, so it pays to spend time up front in this area. If you do, it can set you apart from a standard production designer. You become a collaborator and design strategist. So, my first task is to try to understand how the director intends to use the design to move the story along. This

is crucial because story is the thing that a director (and the audience) cares about most. If we get it wrong - the design is a failure. I like to dive in deep and immerse myself in projects as much as I can, so I'll watch movies the director has done previously to get a feel for their style. I'll read and highlight the entire script of the movie etc. to get a handle on what these designs should (and could) do. The script also gives me specific language and story-points the screen should include. I'll look at production design and concept art to see what style they are going for. If there is already footage filmed, I'll usually get notes and a rough edit/preview of the story to start breaking down. A lot of times this looks like 'Screen 01 does 'A', 'B' and 'C' in x amount of time'.

Dream

Then it's time to put imagination and 'pen to paper' so to speak. I'll work on paper (or the Concepts app on an iPad Pro) to draft a design idea or rough direction. This is where I allow myself to 'draw badly'. Just get the original ideas out there. I've tried skipping this step a few times, and find that I always come back to it. Nothing beats good old fashioned sketching - even if your sketches look like stick figures. These doodles are usually good enough to discuss your direction with your internal team, supervisor etc. This can save a ton of time avoiding going down the wrong path.

Research

After you've got your ideas, do research to fill in your knowledge gaps. Apart from standard google/pinterest/youtube searches, try to find an expert in the subjects. For instance on Robocop, I interviewed several police officers and police trainers on how they work. This gave me tons of insight on the 'real' language they use and how they assess and predict threats. For instance if they are chasing a suspect on foot, they always predict that the suspect will turn right. Apparently when being chased, it's what people do 90% of the time. When interrogating a suspect they always look at the angle of how they stand relative to them - with an eye on the hand/arm that's furthest away from them. This is because the suspect could have a weapon or be winding up for a punch. If they are trying to detect lies they look at the person's perspiration and dilation of their pupils to gauge if they're on drugs. This is stuff I would never have known about and can totally represent in graphically-interesting ways. For my work on Iron man HUDs, I consulted with an A-10 fighter pilot who gave me situational insights into his HUD settings and ways to redesign the layouts to be the ultimate Stark-Level tech. I would say things like, "If you're flying straight up a skyscraper what would be on your HUD?" He'd say, "My ground speed (GS) would be zero, my True Airspeed (TAS) would be high and I'd have all kinds of 'Proximity Alerts' flashing and 'Bitchin' Betty' (their version of Siri) yelling at me 'Pull Up! Pull Up!'" I put all this in the HUD design and was able to sell each part to all who needed to buy off on it. More recently, while consulting for the most advanced next-gen real-world fighter jet HUDs and cockpit displays (NGAD, Next Gen Air Dominance), I've interviewed many pilots flying several generations of the current top-of-the line fighter jets to see how they differed and what could be improved. (There's tons of room for improvement!) All of this kind of research gives you an edge with your designs. You won't need to copy. Your work won't look like the same random micro text and numbers or, worse, like thoughtless clip art that could be slapped over anything. It will have weight and feel functional. It will belong to that movie alone. And that kind of weight and cohesion is really important to modern directors. They understand that today's audiences are getting more and more sophisticated, and they want their films to hold up for years ahead. You can help that by putting in time to mature a design past your first instincts.

Design

Once research is fairly solid, combine your dream phase with your research phase to have a solid base to start designing it out. Just like print design days, for me this means starting with a grid and building on top of that. If you're not good with design, study these three things: Typography, Color Theory, Layout/Composition. They will help you with everything you do from now on.

Present

Typically you'll want to present something that looks like it's 'in' the film. It's difficult for directors, VFX Supervisors, editors, and producers to gauge the success of a design when it's straight out of Illustrator or Photoshop. Most people you're presenting to will not be designers. They need to see it 'in the shot' so to speak. So we'll do what's called 'tempcomps' or 'slapcomps'. Volumetric screens (holograms) are always hard to gauge from stills, so I'll typically do a 3D 'turntable' to show the dimensionality of the design. This allows directors to visualize how they would film it or how it might look comped into a final shot.

What is your typical UI Toolkit?

a) How do you create your concepts? What tools/software do you use?

Initial sketches: I use an app called 'Concepts' for technical drawing on an iPad Pro. Recently I also used Quill and Tilt Brush on an Oculus to sketch volumetric UI's for new Stark-tech. You can import Obj's and draw right over them. This is a great new way to sketch ideas for holographic UIs.

Designs: Illustrator. (I used to design with Photoshop, but

Illustrator is truly that unlimited app you'll never regret mastering and has completely replaced Photoshop for my design phase.)

3D holograms/Volumetric UIs: Cinema 4D. C4D is a 3D app made for designers by designers, and it's become the 'must-know' app for feature film FUI design. Luckily it's not too hard to learn.

Tempcomps: After Effects (Much faster than Photoshop and supports 3D cameras and a final workflow that's much better.) If you're the kind of designer that can design in Illustrator and tempcomp straight in AE, you will be a very valuable team player.

b) How do you create the final execution of the UI or animation that goes to screen? (Or do you hand it over to another team?)

I use After Effects to animate and do final comps. If I'm handing off to another vendor to do final comp it'll be 32b EXR sequences. If it's a 2D screen we will render 'flat'. If it's a volumetric or holographic screen, we'll render a 'to camera' sequence that matches the tracked 3D camera of the scene.

As far as what you're expected to do, every film has a slightly different process that you'll learn from the VFX Supervisor . For instance, sometimes I'll design the master assets only - but most of the time I'm also animating. A lot of the time I'll also composite the designs/animation for direct insertion into the final film. Sometimes I'll just set up the 'Hero' frame which a team of compositors can then match throughout the many shots required. Sometimes it just works out best that way, because just designing graphics often doesn't work when placed into a scene that has motion blur, bokeh, lighting, and different action beats to it. It has to match the pace of the edit. The design has to read clearly even if it's blurred or if characters are walking through it (such as the holograms in Star Wars, Iron Man/Avengers, and Mockingjay). In these types of scenes, I like to design 'in comp', meaning I design based on how it looks in the real 'photographed' scene vs. how it looks in Illustrator.

How do you get a job designing FUI?

It's a great time for it. The demand is just starting to grow so much and will only continue. So many games, films, tv shows, commercials (and AR+VR) are relying on this type of design and animation to tell their story. So, basically it comes down to: Networking and 'doing the work'. Learn as much as you can from every source you can find. Always grow. Then, put your work out there. We're all looking for it. Go to conventions where we're speaking or attending and just come up and meet us. Join my email list (at jayse.tv) and keep in touch. I'm always referring jobs I don't have time to take. It's a constant flow, and I'd love to refer gigs to good people just getting started if they've shown they can pull off some screens and are eager to do what it takes. The way I started was just by asking Mark Coleran if I could just design a widget for him as a free assistant and get him coffee. I also sent him FUI work I had done on my own. It sucked. But it was proof I wasn't just talk.

What is one pro tip you would share?

Learn to design. As in: Design fundamentals. At least the basics. Even if you only want to do compositing, 3D, or animation - your ability to have good design-sense will lift you far above others in the industry in terms of the gigs you get and how much you can charge. And, always, always over-deliver.

Final thoughts

I have a new e-mail list where I'm sharing FUI and next gen UI tips, workflow and behind the scenes of my work. Would love to have you join at www.jayse.tv

INTERVIEW: JÉRÉMIE BENHAMOU

LEAD UI ARTIST AT ACTIVISION / SLEDGEHAMMER GAMES

I've been an interface artist in the videogames industry for almost 10 years. First at EA, Ubisoft, then Activision. I currently work on this year's Call of Duty's interfaces.

Credits include: Call of Duty: WWII, Call of Duty: Advanced Warfare, Dead Space 2, Dead Space 3, Assassins Creed: Unity, Rainbow Six: Siege

Website: jeremie.tv
Behance: behance.net/jeremietv

What does your typical process/workflow look like when creating a game UI?

1. Knowing the game, understanding the gameplay, creative, and art directions

2. Research: Collect references, inspiration material (I personally get most of my visual references from movies)

3. Styleguide: Define a direction, colors, fonts, legacy, layouts,...

4. Concepts / mockups: Based on the styleguide rules

5. Exporting assets from mockups

6. Implementing assets in game

What is your typical UI Toolkit?

a) How do you create your concepts? What tools/software do you use?

I use Adobe Photoshop all the time, not so much Illustrator. Maya for 3D assets, either modeling, or importing game assets to edit them and export them in a friendly format, depending on my needs.

After Effects for animated mockups. I often capture gameplay footage with "Fraps" and compose interfaces mockups over it.

b) How do you create the final execution of the UI or animation that goes to screen? (Or do you hand it over to another team?)

For diegetic interfaces, we mainly use 2 types of interfaces:
You can create an animation with After Effects, then export to Quicktime, convert to bink (or whatever format your game engine supports), and hand over to texture artists who will use your video in a 'cinematic material'.

The other type is a TGA flipbook, much lighter for small loops: each frame of your animation is a small square of one big texture. Attached is an example: the Advanced Warfare loading logo animation; a 2048x2048px texture containing each frame of a 120-frame animation. The engine will read each frame sequentially and loop them.

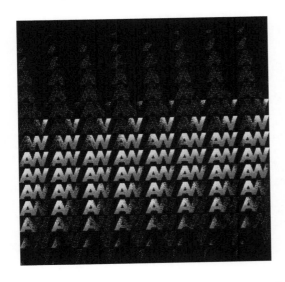

Non-diegetic interfaces require more work: Once your Photoshop mockup is done, you export all individual assets as TGA or PNG images, and either hand them to UI engineers for them to implement, or use them in an in-house UI tool, placing each asset in the "box" designed to host them.

What's the best way to get a job designing UI for games?

Build a portfolio and publish it on Behance and LinkedIn. Recruiters use these 2 platforms extensively to find new UI profiles.

It's better if your LinkedIn title matches exactly what the recruiter is looking for. You could browse the "Jobs" sections on your favorite companies (the ones you want to enter), and mimic their wording for your title.

From my experience, applying directly through studios' websites is useless.

What is one pro tip you would share?

If you apply somewhere and don't hear back, it is probably a matter of bad timing between the company's needs and your application. Try again and again, reach out through LinkedIn and email.
School degrees don't really matter. A different background (no video games in your portfolio, for instance) is not a big issue.

INTERVIEW: JOHN LEPORE

PRINCIPLE, CHIEF CREATIVE DIRECTOR AT PERCEPTION

John LePore has his dream job.

Leading the creative team at Perception, an award-winning creative consultancy based in New York City, John's career is focused on a realm that resembles his childhood sketchbooks brought to life. His workday consists of contributing imaginative concepts to blockbuster films, and solving problems for some of the most exciting products in technology. Always excited to share his craft, John frequently presents at industry conferences (Siggraph, NAB), and works as a product specialist and evangelist for Maxon Computer, the creators of Cinema 4D.

John is always striving to find a closer integration between his career and his life's work as a father, husband, and racing driver.

Credits include: Batman V Superman: Dawn of Justice, Captain America: Civil War, Iron Man 2, The Avengers, Robocop, Thor: The Dark World, The Europa Report

Website: experienceperception.com
Twitter: www.twitter.com/johnnymotion,
www.twitter.com/exp_perception

What does your typical process/workflow look like when creating FUI?

During the conceptual (pre-production) process:

- Finding emerging real-world tech, R&D experiments etc, and extrapolating those appropriately into the future (think: MIT Media Lab etc).

- Determining if these technologies work in the story being told:
  - Is this an appropriately advanced technology (how far into the future should it feel)?
  - Does this match the personality of the characters, the environment, the story as a whole?
  - Does the tech allow for exceptionally clear communication of key story points?
  - Does the tech encourage the actors to "perform" while interacting? (gesture, voice commands, etc)
  - Does the tech enable the filmmakers to tell their story in new ways, solve logistical problems etc

During Design & execution:

- Start by experimenting with style-frames to discover visual themes that resonate (and can appropriately scale).

- Collaborating with filmmakers to ensure that we are not just solving their potential problems, but also enabling them to simplify and streamline the storytelling process.

Focus on key story points to ensure communication is clear— strong legibility, directing the viewer's eye to the most relevant information.

What is your typical FUI Toolkit?

a) How do you create your concepts? What tools/software do you use?

The typical approach would likely be

1. Sketching general concepts on paper
2. Designing basic elements in Illustrator
3. Creating 3D elements in Cinema 4D
4. Merging them together in Photoshop or After Effects
5. Tweaking colors, glows, compositing effects in Photoshop or After Effects

However I find that I bounce between all of the programs and platforms in no particular order— It's very easy to get caught up in deep minutiae of icons and widgets in Illustrator, and I find it helps to step way back and do some quick compositing tests that may make me change the way I am making details. Usually when I'm about halfway done with something being built from a myriad of heavy 2D and 3D elements, I will switch over to pen and paper to drastically change the overall composition. This helps to make bigger, better decisions without being married to a 200-layer layout or complex 3D render.

FUI designs can quickly become a swamp of hyper-detailed elements that serve no purpose but to add complexity and texture. If you find yourself getting lost making these little details, it never hurts to save what you are working on, and start a clean new comp. You can always find a purpose later for the little widgets you've been obsessing over.

b) How do you create the final execution of the UI or animation that goes to screen? (Or do you hand it over to another team?)

Our typical process is to integrate elements into footage plates in Nuke and occasionally After Effects. On occasion we will hand off elements for integration by another studio, particularly if they are handling other effects work in the same shot.

How do you get a job designing FUI?

On a least 3 occasions, I have hired someone who I have seen posting FUI personal projects on Twitter or Pinterest.

What is one pro tip you would share?

Often you have a bold, clear message made to convey a plot point, surrounded by greebles (superfluous, busy details to simulate complexity or sophistication). The goal should be that any of these secondary elements should be serving as part of an overall system, and provide clues as to how the technology works. Animation can pull a lot of weight here - seeing how the elements move in relationship to each other. When done properly, every audience member thinks they were the only ones observant enough to get it.

INTERVIEW: JORGE ALMEIDA

USER INTERFACE DESIGNER, ANIMATOR, AND FINE ARTIST

Jorge Almeida has spent 14 years working in the film industry as a user interface designer and animator. He has been credited as lead interface designer on such films as Minority Report, The Italian Job, Mission Impossible: Ghost Protocol and Star Trek Into Darkness. He has also done some illustration work, with his drawings being featured in the end-title sequence for the film Sherlock Holmes.

He is currently working with Microsoft as a UI Designer and Animator for one of the Hololens teams.

Credits include: Minority Report, Star Trek Into Darkness, The Dark Knight Rises, Mission Impossible: Ghost Protocol, Iron Man 2, Microsoft Future Vision 2015

Website: jorgeonline.me
Instagram: instagram.com/almeidaartist

What does your typical process/workflow look like when creating FUI?

After meeting with the Production Designer or Director, I will usually do my own research and sketch notes or ideas on paper. I will also start putting shapes, colors, and fonts together in Adobe Illustrator just to get the process going. Hopefully by then I'm starting to get a pretty clear idea in my head of how the interface should feel. It helps me to come up with some type of metaphor or concept that I'm trying to illustrate, so that the design becomes a translation of that idea instead of just a bunch of shapes on the screen. Even going as far back as "Minority Report," I tried to imagine the giant precog interface as an autopsy table and the precog data as a giant organism. I don't know that this comes across in the final execution, but it helps me personally to connect to my work and hopefully come up with something that feels original.

The next meeting with production is when I would begin showing rough designs, as well as any reference I may have found. Subsequent meetings are about refining the style and emphasizing story points. What needs to be remembered in film UI is that you are painting a small part of a much larger painting. It is more like set design than UI design. In real-world UI, you have a specific number of buttons, functions, menus, etc and the objective becomes how to build a design that includes all of those elements in a way that is logical and clear to the user. In film UI you are designing around specific story points. The interface doesn't need to be functional to the audience, only to the character onscreen. In real-world UI the objective is often to make the design simpler and cleaner, to make it easier for the user. But in film it can be the opposite. The viewer is watching the character and how they interact with the interface. For this reason, the more complex you make the interface- the smarter or more competent the character can look.

What is your typical FUI Toolkit?

a) How do you create your concepts? What tools/software do you use?

My early concepts are normally built using Illustrator, Photoshop, and After Effects. Beginning in Illustrator, I will block in shapes, and mix and match colors, fonts, etc. I have a couple of files with grids, blocks of text or gradients that I'll sometimes grab from if I need to. I will also import thumbnails sketches, images, or backgrounds that I created in Photoshop. I try to keep elements separated into as many layers as possible. I will turn on/off the various layers, mixing and matching until I land on something I like.

When I reach a stopping point, I will export my file as a layered psd. In Photoshop I'll add effects, as well as any additional rendered elements into the design before I present to production. That would include 3D elements built by other members of the team, or elements provided to us by production. In the past, I've also created many 3D elements in After Effects using flat graphics in 3D space. I'm also finally learning Cinema 4D, and am starting to incorporate my own 3D into my concepts.

I like to save off as many versions as possible in both Illustrator and Photoshop. I will then use Adobe Bridge to preview images and narrow down choices. It's especially useful because of its ability to preview Illustrator files as thumbnails. I can then rate and organize my favorites to show production.

Although I don't start with much of a toolkit, I usually have a full set by the time we reach post-production. By then we've built a full collection of UI graphics and looping animations that played on set. By the time I reach the end of a project, I'm usually doing much of my designing directly in After Effects- allowing me to work with graphics that are already animated.

b) How do you create the final execution of the UI or animation that goes to screen? (Or do you hand it over to another team?)

In the past, I've animated most of my own designs- so I've prepped most of my own files for compositing. This normally involves rendering hi-res frame sequences, along with a quicktime preview of the animation. I will also provide any approved style frames or comps for reference.

If the animation is being composited onto a monitor, I would provide a single flat frame sequence with no alpha. If the animation is being composited onto glass or floating in space, I would separate the animation into layers and render each element individually with alpha channels. This way the compositor has as much flexibility as possible when dialing in the final look.

How do you get a job designing FUI?

Learn to animate your own designs. Good motion artists are harder to find, so it might help you get in the door.

What is one pro tip you would share?

Work in greyscale as much as possible. If the design does not work in black and white, then it will not work in color. I normally create a desaturation layer at the top of all my design and motion comps which allows me to quickly see my design in greyscale. For Adobe Illustrator, I create a white square on the top layer of my comp and change the transparency mode to "Saturation."

INTERVIEW: RYAN RAFFERTY-PHELAN

MOTION DESIGNER AT TERRITORY STUDIO

Ryan Rafferty-Phelan is a designer, director and animator based in London, working in feature film, commercials and branding.

Working at Territory Studio since 2013, he's had the pleasure to work on many fantastic projects with the team, ranging from blockbuster smashes Guardians of the Galaxy, Avengers Age of Ultron, Mission Impossible V to leading projects with LA director Saman Kesh and for Australia's premier creative technology festival, PauseFest.

Credits include: Avengers Age of Ultron, Mission Impossible V, Agent 47, Guardians of the Galaxy

Website: territorystudio.com, ryanraffertyphelan.com
Pinterest: pinterest.com/ryanrphelan
Twitter: twitter.com/ryanrphelan

What does your typical process/workflow look like when creating FUI?

The first step I take is to digest the creative brief, which will typically come from the Production Designer/Supervising Art Director on the film.

The brief doesn't necessarily come in document form, this can be notes from a call or just some loose thoughts depending on how much information we've been given at the start to work with. I'll read through the script if it has been provided, and pick out the key components that will need to be reflected either in design or functionality, also the ones I think can be enhanced by FUI. I'll then start out by pulling some very surface references for a few different directions that feel appropriate. References generally serve as the foundation for communication between myself, the Creative Director and the production team based onset. These references are put together in a deck and shared with the director and their team, opening up the discussion and enabling us to get to the essence of what they want to achieve aesthetically.

Depending on the scale of the project and time allowed for concepting, I may then refine the references to provide a narrower focus and clearer indication of the direction. It's good to have a strong base to constantly refer back to and question if what you're creating has the qualities of the elements you've drawn from the reference material or that the director feels particularly strongly about.

The next step at this point is to start by creating styleframes. This involves laying down line work in Illustrator, establishing typography and then building up layers of treatment in Photoshop or After Effects. These style frames are the next thing the client will see, and a process of feedback and development will begin until the client is happy with the direction. This process may sometimes require jumping into animation early on so the client can get a feel for how things will move which a still frame doesn't necessarily indicate.

At this point it really depends on the nature of the project. If there's a lot of screens that are part of a particular look and style, this is a good point to start developing a library of assets or framework in Illustrator that will form the basis of that "OS". If the screens are very story specific, the Director will want to see how those story beats are going to be tackled, so we'll design around those beats and look to get that locked in as best we can. Often the Director will be tweaking and adjusting the story through-out so the beats may change but it's important to get the basis of them down.

The project transitions into the production phase at this point where the concept has generally been worked out, the team will often ramp up, bringing on more designers and animators or 3D artists depending on what's required.

What is your typical FUI Toolkit?

a) How do you create your concepts? What tools/software do you use?

Typically, the standard tools – Illustrator, Photoshop, After Effects & Cinema 4D

b) How do you create the final execution of the UI or animation that goes to screen? (Or do you hand it over to another team?)

I use Illustrator for graphic design work, this includes the line work and typographic elements of the UI. Cinema 4D is perfect for any 3D elements that feature in the screen, whether that's visualising something in the film or creating interesting data widgets or particle based systems. Photoshop is then used to bind the graphics together, adding layers of treatment, texture, color adjustments, curves, levels etc to create the final look. I'll then either import the Photoshop file to use in After Effects or import the illustrator linework and start animating straight from that - adding treatment layers later in After Effects.

Finished files are rendered and delivered to playback on-set if they're going to be shot in camera (more often than not they are) otherwise I'll either deliver renders to our VFX team that will comp them into shots, or we'll hand them over to the VFX vendor that is comping for them to integrate.

How do you get a job designing FUI?

My advice for someone wanting to get into the FUI industry would be to start off by really understanding basic graphic design fundamentals. These skills will serve you throughout your career, far more than any particular piece of software currently in vogue. Have a love for design in general, but more specifically - layout, typography, color, hierarchy, space, symmetry, contrast, grids, balance and texture. Photography and film are great to have an appreciation of, understanding storytelling and narrative and how those apply to your craft are essential to being a successful designer for film or games.

Attending college or university whilst by no means essential, can provide a platform and a stop gap for you to find what aspect of design really grabs you. I studied Digital Media Design at LCC (London

College of Communication), part of University of The Arts London, and found it really gave me the opportunity to explore different avenues of design.

Your portfolio is the most essential tool you have in getting yourself a job. Make sure you have a website and it is up to date. Leave out the old bits that don't reflect your current abilities and try to make sure that the bits that do reflect the type of work you'd like more of, are front and centre stage.

Finally, get out there and introduce yourself to people. Get involved in the design community through the many different social avenues that are available, including Twitter, Pinterest, Instagram, etc. LinkedIn can be useful but probably more so when you have a some experience to offer. Don't be afraid to phone studios too! I got my first internship in my second year of Uni by phoning the studio directly. I was determined to not waste the summer and wanted an internship. After phoning lots of studios and getting through to receptionists, I was fortunate enough to get straight through to the owner and he invited me in for chat. That was where I got my start, one phone call.

What is one pro tip you would share?

It's an obvious one but, people buy people. If you want to get far in anything, being sociable, making conversation and making friends in the industry are key. I definitely wouldn't have had the wonderful opportunities I've had in my career so far if it wasn't for the people around me that I've been fortunate enough to meet and get to know along the way. People generally want to work with people they get on well with and will prioritise them over others they don't know so well.

USEFUL LINKS AND TUTORIALS

H ERE ARE SOME RESOURCES THAT MIGHT help you get started.

1. Learn Squared

In-depth video tutorial courses run by an amazing cast of industry leading artists. There are several courses available but the one most relevant here is Ash Thorp's UI and Data Design for Film course. Visit the link to find out more, including a student gallery showing what can be achieved upon taking the course.

- **Ash Thorp's UI and Data Design for Film course**
  learnsquared.com/courses/ui-and-data-design-film

- **Learn Squared site**
  learnsquared.com

2. Maxon Cineversity - FUI series

An online training and resource site for Cinema 4D users, that includes a special tutorial series by Perception focusing on FUI.

There are three tutorials available free to public, and there are a few others that require a subscription.

There are also some interesting talks by FUI designers recorded at NAB and SIGGRAPH, which are worth checking out too.

Perception's FUI series
cineversity.com/vidplaylist/the_perception_guide_to_fui

NAB and SIGGRAPH talks
cineversity.com/learn/fui

3. Aescripts

An excellent source of tutorials and handy tools for After Effects, including many resources useful and specific to FUI.

Aescripts tutorials
aescripts.com/learn/cat/tutorials

Aescripts site
aescripts.com

4. Motionographer - Step by Step series

An amazing source of inspiration within the area of motion graphics. Very relevant to the FUI space, particularly from a film, storytelling and design point of view. They've recently launched the Step by Step series that focuses on breaking down how industry-leading creatives work on a daily basis. This is very closely related field to FUI and the designers for both share very similar workflows and skillsets.

Motionographer
motionographer.com

Step by Step series
motionographer.com/tag/step-by-step

5. Video Copilot

A collaborative resource for training, design tools and artists. Primarily focusing on motion graphics and effects, this is an amazing resource offering an abundance of free high quality tutorials.

Video Copilot tutorials
videocopilot.net

6. Greyscale Gorilla

A training and resource site dedicated to Cinema 4D. Really professional free tutorials that teach you how to do some really amazing things in 3D.

GSG tutorials
greyscalegorilla.com/tutorials

7. Ian Water's Mash Tutorials

Creator of Mash, an Autodesk extension for Maya (3D software) that focuses on procedural effects, Ian Waters provides useful tutorials, many of which focus on elements of FUI. If you use Maya, this might be a handy way to incorporate it into your FUI workflow.

Ian's Mash Tutorials (click on YouTube in the menu)
ianwaters.co.uk/wp/

8. FUI on reddit

Here's a wonderful resource for FUI news. There's quite an active community growing here and it's a great place to chat to fellow FUI enthusiasts.

FUI subreddit
reddit.com/r/FUI

9. Jayse Hansen's mailing list

Jayse has started a mailing list to discuss FUI and share some of his behind the scenes FUI tips. Head over to his website to sign up: www. jayse.tv

THANK YOU!

I HOPE YOU'VE ENJOYED THIS GUIDE AS much as I loved writing it for you. I've really tried to share all the gold that I've discovered throughout the years in this. I can't thank you enough for your continued support of HUDS+GUS.

I appreciate each and every one of you for taking time out of your day to read this.

If I can ask just one thing, I would love to hear what you think about this guide.

Please rate this book and leave a comment on Amazon, it would really help me out!

Or if you'd rather say hello on Twitter, my handle is @hudsandguis

Best of luck and I wish you all the best in pursuing your passions! Know that I'll be cheering you on!

ABOUT THE AUTHOR

Jono Yuen is an award winning designer, illustrator, creative director and accidental writer who has been in the digital creative industry for over 10+ years. Formerly Head of Art at Tribal DDB Worldwide (Australia) for over 6 of those years. Specialising in creating intelligent and enjoyable digital experiences, his work has been recognised globally with numerous accolades and awards across brands in various business sectors. His work has been exhibited locally and internationally, most recently in London, Rijeka, Tokyo and Time Square, New York, as well as being published in various publications around the world.

Jono is also the founder of Future User Interface design community HUDS+GUIS, where he helps bring awareness to the best work in the field and the artists behind them. He speaks on the topics of Future User Interfaces, digital experience design and design mentoring.

Jono now focuses his energy on helping young designers reach their goals, with projects like HUDS+GUIS and some new projects currently in the works! Jono lives in Melbourne, Australia with his wife Natalie and his son.

To learn more about Jono, go to:
jonoyuen.com/about

ABOUT HUDS+GUIS

HUDS+GUIS (hudsandguis.com) is a resource run by Jono Yuen that brings together the most creative examples of UI design with the artists that create them. With an emphasis on Fictional User Interfaces (FUI), the work can come from films, television, games, concept designs and real world developments.

The goal of the site is to provide inspiration and insight to allow designers and creators to develop better UI for the future. It also aims to shed light on a fairly unrecognised, niche area of design, and be a source of information, news and helpful advice.

HUDS+GUIS now takes on the role of supporting designers wanting to find out more about the industry and how to improve their work.

To keep in touch, join the HUDS+GUIS mailing list for the most up to date news, resources and opportunities.

Go to hudsandguis.com/mailing-list

Or contact them any time with feedback, questions, news or just to say hi!

info@hudsanguis.com

Disclaimer

The information contained in this guide is for informational purposes only.

Any advice that I give is my opinion based on my own experience. You should always seek the advice of a professional before acting on something that I have published or recommended.

The material in this guide may include information, products, or services by third parties. Third Party Materials comprise the products and opinions expressed by their owners. As such, I do not assume responsibility or liability for any Third Party material or opinions.

The publication of such Third Party Materials does not constitute my guarantee of any information, instruction, opinion, products, or services contained within the Third Party Material. The use of recommended Third Party Material does not guarantee any success and/or earnings related to you or your business. Publication of such Third Party Material is simply a recommendation and an expression of my own opinion of that material.

No part of this publication shall be reproduced, transmitted, or sold in whole or in part in any form, without the prior written consent of the author. All trademarks and registered trademarks appearing in this guide are the property of their respective owners.

Users of this guide are advised to do their own due diligence when it comes to making business decisions and all information, products, and services that have been provided should be independently verified by your own qualified professionals. By reading this guide, you agree that myself and my company is not responsible for the success or failure of your business decisions relating to any information presented in this guide.

Printed in Great Britain
by Amazon